Children's
FIRST
Book of
LONG LONG AGO

Children's
FIRST
Book of

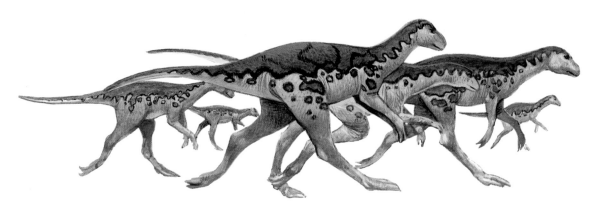

p

Author and Editor
Neil Morris

Projects created by
Ting Morris

Art Direction
Full Steam Ahead Ltd

Designer
Branka Surla

Project Management
Rosie Alexander

Artwork commissioned by
Branka Surla

Picture Research
Rosie Alexander, Kate Miles, Elaine Willis, Yannick Yago

Editorial Assistant
Lynne French

Additional editorial help from
Suzanne Airey, Hilary Bird, Paul Kilgour, Jenny Sharman

Editorial Director
Jim Miles

The publishers would like to thank the following people for their help:
Jenni Cozens, Pat Crisp, Ian Paulyn

This is a Parragon Book
This edition published in 2000

Parragon
Queen Street House
4 Queen Street
Bath BA1 1HE, UK

Copyright © Parragon 1998

Produced by Miles Kelly Publishing Ltd
Unit 11, Bardfield Centre, Great Bardfield, Essex CM7 4SL

British Library Cataloguing-in-Publication Data
A catalogue record for this book is available from the British Library

ISBN 0-75254-297-4

Printed in Dubai, U.A.E.

Contents

How to use this book

In this book, every page is filled with information on the sort of topics that you will enjoy reading about.

Information is given in photographs and illustrations, as well as in words. All the pictures are explained by captions, to tell you what you are looking at and to give even more detailed facts.

Beautiful photographs have been specially chosen to bring each subject to life. The caption triangle points to the right photograph.

A New Words box appears on every double-page spread. This list explains some difficult words and technical terms.

The cartoons throughout the book are not always meant to be taken too seriously! They are supposed to be fun, but the text that goes with them gives real information.

Project boxes describe craft activities related to the topic. These are things to make or simple experiments to do. The photograph helps to show you what to do, and is there to inspire you to have a go! But remember, some of the activities can be quite messy, so put old newspaper down first. Always use round-ended scissors, and ask an adult for help if you are unsure of something or need sharp tools or materials.

The main text on each double-page spread gives a short introduction to that particular topic. Every time you turn the page, you will find a new topic.

Illustrations are clear and simple, and sometimes they are cut away so that you can see inside things. The triangle at the beginning of the caption text points to the illustration concerned.

Captions beginning with a symbol give extra pieces of information that you will find interesting.

Long Long Ago

The amazing story of life on Earth takes us right back to the early days of our planet. In recent times we have learned a great deal about life's history, including the fascinating period that we call the Age of Dinosaurs.

For many millions of years, the land was dominated by meat-eating and plant-eating dinosaurs, while plesiosaurs swam in the oceans and pterosaurs flew in the skies. Then all these amazing reptiles, many of them giants, died out, to be replaced by mammals who, in prehistoric times, came to dominate the planet. Through our study of fossils, we can now piece together how this all came about.

Early Life

Life on Earth has been developing and changing over billions of years. Scientists now believe that the simplest forms of life began in the world's oceans, probably over three billion years ago.

△ **This is blue-green algae,** one of the simplest forms of life, seen through a microscope. It is made up of a skin surrounding a watery "soup", and has no complicated parts.

We can only guess what the very first plants and animals looked like. But we think that many early sea animals had soft bodies, without shells, bones or other hard parts. They included jellyfish, different kinds of worms and other creatures related to starfishes.

◁ **These jellyfish,** sea pens and worms lived in the world's oceans about 650 million years ago. They were mainly on the seabed.

NEW WORDS
algae Plants that grow in the sea, without true stems, leaves or roots.
jellyfish A sea animal with an umbrella-shaped body like jelly.
sea pen A feather-shaped sea animal related to jellyfish.
starfish A sea animal that has the shape of a five-pointed star.

△ **The shallow coastal areas** of the early oceans were full of green, brown and red algae, which we call seaweeds. Today, there are about 7,000 different kinds of seaweed. Most are found in warm, tropical waters.

How old are sharks?
The ancestors of today's sharks were swimming in the seas about 400 million years ago. They are one of the oldest animal groups with backbones still alive today.

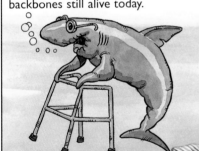

△ **Fast-moving, armour-plated fish** like this Coccosteus ruled the seas about 370 million years ago. A typical Coccosteus was about 40 cm long, and had sharp bony ridges and tusks inside its strong jaws. It could easily catch and eat slower-moving shellfish.

The first fishes had a head, a backbone and a tail, but no fins or jaws. They could not swim fast and sucked food into their mouths instead of biting it.

▽ **Scientists** thought that Coelacanths died out about 70 million years ago. But in 1938, a fisherman caught one in the Indian Ocean. These ancient fish grow up to 2 m long.

Evolution

Most scientists believe that different forms of life on Earth developed and changed very slowly over millions of years. They call this gradual process "evolution".

Animals and plants have evolved with time, as one generation followed another. Tiny changes in one generation built up to big changes over millions of years.

As the world changed, it suited some animals better than others. Those animals which adapted easily to their surroundings did well and became more plentiful, while others died out over time.

▽ **In 1832** Charles Darwin arrived in South America. There he found fossils of extinct animals. His studies of these and living animals led him to develop his famous theory of evolution.

NEW WORDS

adapt To adjust to different conditions.
evolution The gradual change and development of life over millions of years.
fossil Former living thing preserved in rock.
extinct Not existing any more, having died out.

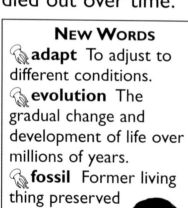

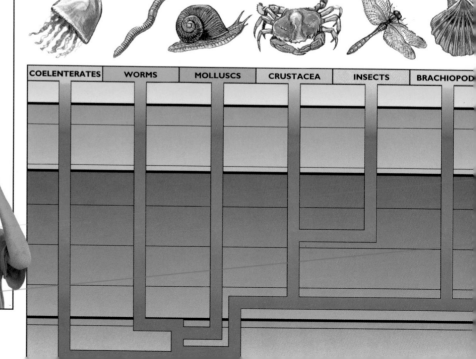

COELENTERATES	WORMS	MOLLUSCS	CRUSTACEA	INSECTS	BRACHIOPOD

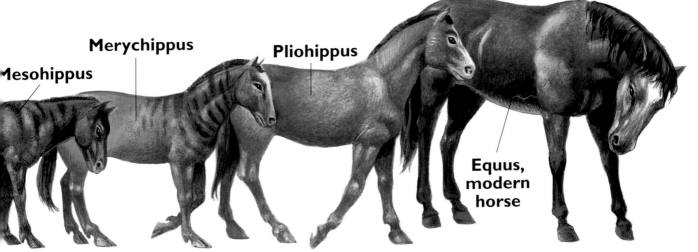

Mesohippus

Merychippus

Pliohippus

Equus, modern horse

△ **The horse** has developed over 50 million years. The first horse, Hyracotherium, lived in swampy forests and was as big as a modern fox. Equus has been around for about three million years.

Charles Darwin (1809-82), the famous scientist, sailed right around the world in a ship called *The Beagle* for five years.

▽ **This chart** shows how life has developed over millions of years. Human beings only appeared in the surprisingly recent past.

△ **A giraffe** has a long neck, an anteater has a long nose, and a monkey has very long arms. All these features developed to help the animals feed and live.

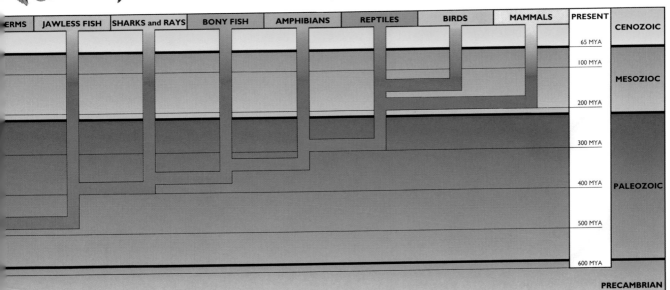

ERMS	JAWLESS FISH	SHARKS and RAYS	BONY FISH	AMPHIBIANS	REPTILES	BIRDS	MAMMALS	PRESENT	
									CENOZOIC
								65 MYA	
								100 MYA	
									MESOZIOC
								200 MYA	
								300 MYA	
								400 MYA	PALEOZOIC
								500 MYA	
								600 MYA	
									PRECAMBRIAN

The Age of Amphibians

About 360 million years ago, some sea creatures left the water and crawled out onto land. Already there were many different fish in the sea, as well as plants and insects on land.

By now some animals could live on land and in water. We call these animals amphibians, which means "having a double life". Steamy swamps and forests were an ideal place for them to live. Amphibians laid their eggs in water. The eggs hatched into swimming tadpoles, and when they became adults, they moved onto the land. This is exactly how amphibians such as frogs and toads live today.

swampy forest

peat bog

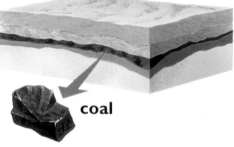

coal

△ **Dead leaves** and branches formed layers of plant material in the swampy forests of the early amphibians. This made peat, and when this was covered by rocks, the pressure turned it into coal.

▷ **Ichthyostega** was one of the first amphibians. It was about 1 m long. Giant dragonflies and many other insects lived among the tall, treelike ferns.

◁ **Ancient coal** has provided us with knowledge about the past, as well as fuel. Some leaves survived intact as the coal was formed and made fossils like this one.

▷ **This North American bullfrog** is a good example of a modern amphibian. Bullfrogs spend most of their time near water. All frogs breathe through lungs, as well as through their skin. Today there are about 4,000 different kinds of amphibians round the world, including frogs, toads, newts and salamanders.

Early amphibians were much bigger than they are today. The early giants died out about 200 million years ago. But there is one exception, a giant salamander, which lives in China and can grow to a length of 1.8 m.

PREHISTORIC LANDSCAPE
Use a large cereal box as a base, with the lid as a background. Cut and tape the box, line it with blue paper, cut out a volcano and stick it on. Use tissue paper for giant ferns, and put cellophane over some blue paper for a lake. Colour some sand green with food colouring and sprinkle it on the base. Build rocks with stones and cones, and add a plasticine dinosaur.

NEW WORDS
amphibian An animal that lives on land but lays its eggs in water.
dragonfly An insect with a long body and two pairs of thin wings.
peat Rotted plant material in the ground.
swamp An area of wet, low and marshy ground.

Early Reptiles

Many millions of years ago, in the world's swampy forests, could be found the first reptiles. They were small, lizard-like animals, that fed mainly on insects and worms.

But reptiles are different from amphibians in one important way: reptiles can live on land all the time. Their eggs can also be laid on land, as they are protected by a leathery shell. Reptiles became the world's first true land-dwellers.

Over millions of years, many different sorts of scaly-skinned reptiles evolved. Some were very large and some were small, some ate plants and some fed on other animals. At first they had legs at the sides of their bodies, like many lizards today. Later, some reptiles evolved so that their legs were more underneath their bodies, which meant they could run faster!

Reptiles had lost any dependance on water to lay their eggs and so they could take over the land. They could even live in hot dry deserts far from the sea.

△ **Mesosaurs** were reptiles that found their food in the sea. They went back to the water to catch fish. They had needle-like teeth that interlocked when they closed their jaws.

The first reptiles appeared about 300 million years ago. By 280 million years ago, the amphibians were becoming less common and there were many different kinds and sizes of reptiles.

The name "reptile" comes from the Latin word for "crawl".

Which were the ruling reptiles?
The archosaurs, or "ruling reptiles", developed after the early reptiles. Some looked like crocodiles. Others could stand up on their legs, like the later dinosaurs.

Today there are about 6,500 different kinds of reptiles all over the world. These include snakes, crocodiles, alligators, lizards and turtles.

> **NEW WORDS**
> **interlock** To fit in between each other.
> **reptile** An animal with a waterproof skin covered in horny scales, who depends on its surroundings to keep warm.
> **yolk** The yellow part inside an eggshell.

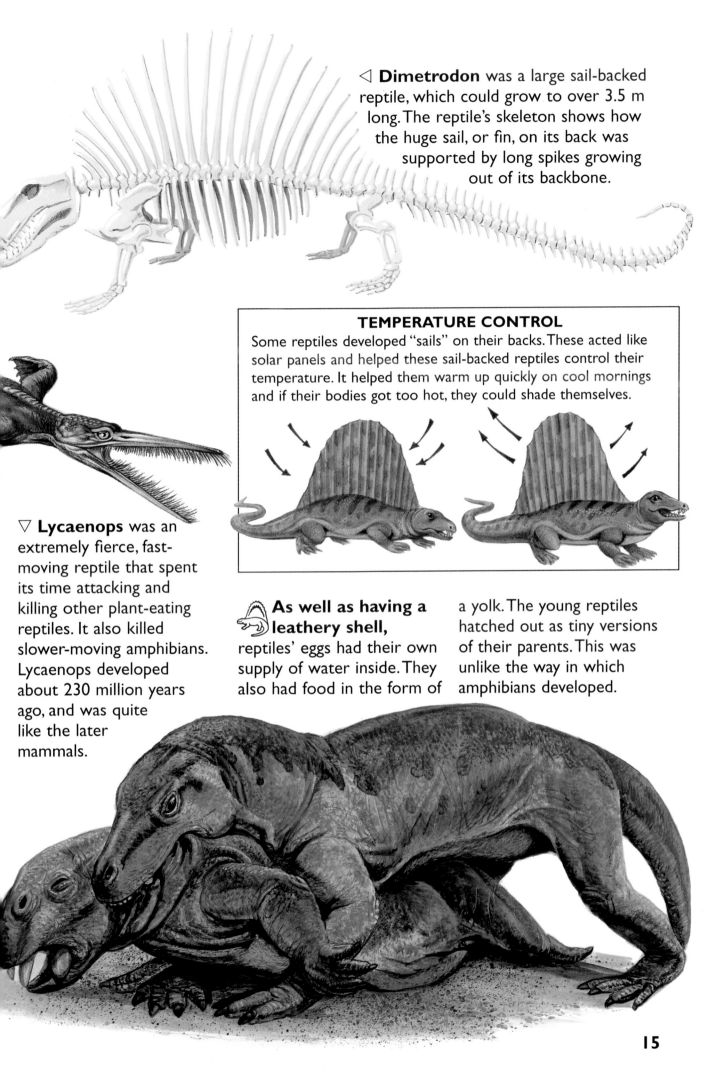

◁ **Dimetrodon** was a large sail-backed reptile, which could grow to over 3.5 m long. The reptile's skeleton shows how the huge sail, or fin, on its back was supported by long spikes growing out of its backbone.

TEMPERATURE CONTROL

Some reptiles developed "sails" on their backs. These acted like solar panels and helped these sail-backed reptiles control their temperature. It helped them warm up quickly on cool mornings and if their bodies got too hot, they could shade themselves.

▽ **Lycaenops** was an extremely fierce, fast-moving reptile that spent its time attacking and killing other plant-eating reptiles. It also killed slower-moving amphibians. Lycaenops developed about 230 million years ago, and was quite like the later mammals.

As well as having a leathery shell, reptiles' eggs had their own supply of water inside. They also had food in the form of a yolk. The young reptiles hatched out as tiny versions of their parents. This was unlike the way in which amphibians developed.

LIZARD HIPS AND BIRD HIPS

Scientists have divided dinosaurs into two main groups, according to the shapes of their hips. One group, including Tyrannosaurus (above right), had hips shaped like those of a modern lizard. The other group, which included Stegosaurus (below), had hips like a bird.

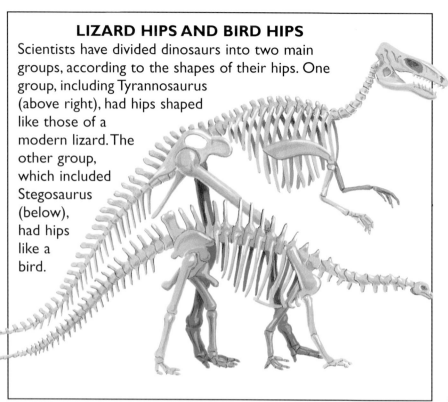

All the meat-eating dinosaurs and big four-legged plant-eaters were lizard-hipped. The later bird-hipped dinosaurs were all plant-eaters.

◁ **This scientist** is working at Dinosaur National Monument, in Utah, USA. More than 5,000 dinosaur fossils have been found there. The most common remains have been those of Stegosaurus.

▷ **This barrel-bodied plant-eater** used to be called Brontosaurus. But then it was found to be the same as earlier fossils called Apatosaurus, so the first name was chosen for this creature.

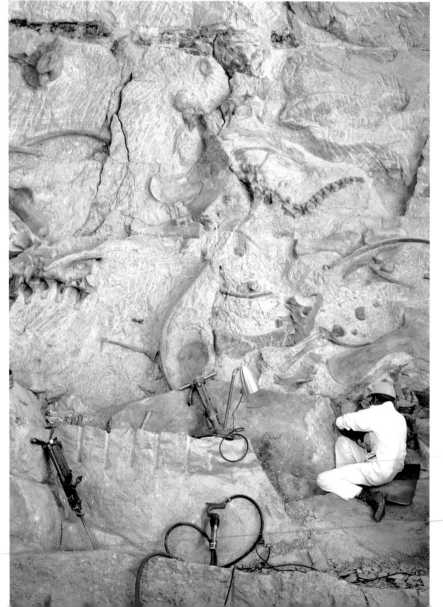

Dinosaurs

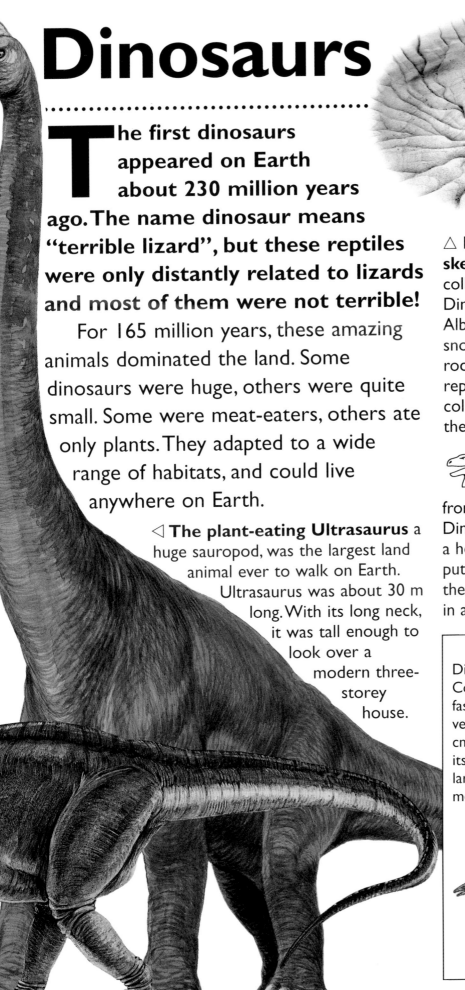

The first dinosaurs appeared on Earth about 230 million years ago. The name dinosaur means "terrible lizard", but these reptiles were only distantly related to lizards and most of them were not terrible!

For 165 million years, these amazing animals dominated the land. Some dinosaurs were huge, others were quite small. Some were meat-eaters, others ate only plants. They adapted to a wide range of habitats, and could live anywhere on Earth.

◁ **The plant-eating Ultrasaurus** a huge sauropod, was the largest land animal ever to walk on Earth. Ultrasaurus was about 30 m long. With its long neck, it was tall enough to look over a modern three-storey house.

△ **Hundreds of dinosaur skeletons** have been collected in the badlands of Dinosaur Provincial Park, in Alberta, Canada. Rain and snow have worn away the rocks, uncovering the reptile remains. Dinosaur collectors first rushed to the area in the early 1900s.

Today's scientists move large bones from regions such as Dinosaur Provincial Park by a helicopter or truck. They put the pieces together, and the skeletons are displayed in a nearby museum.

SIZES

Dinosaurs came in all sizes. Compsognathus was a small, fast-moving, meat-eater with very sharp teeth. It was 70 cm to 1.4 m long, including its long tail. It probably ate large insects, lizards and mouse-like mammals.

Meat-eating Dinosaurs

The dinosaur carnivores, or meat-eaters, were powerfully built animals. They walked upright on their two back legs, and their shorter arms ended in hands with clawed fingers.

The big meat-eaters, such as Tyrannosaurus, had a huge head on a short neck. They had very strong, sharp teeth. Nearly all meat-eaters had a long, muscular tail, which they carried straight out behind them. This helped them to balance their heavy weight. Their strong back legs made meat-eaters the fastest of all the dinosaurs.

△ **Oviraptor** had a tall crest on the top of its head. This bird-like creature fed on other dinosaurs' eggs, which it scooped up in its three-fingered hands and cracked open with its strong jaws. Oviraptors were about 2 m long.

Which was fastest?
We don't know how fast dinosaurs could run, but scientists think Struthiomimus was one of the fastest. It was 4 m long, looked like an ostrich and may have reached speeds of 50 kph.

◁ **Allosaurus** was one of the biggest meat-eaters before Tyrannosaurus. It was 11 m long. We don't know what colour dinosaurs were, but some might have been brightly coloured.

Ostrich-like Struthiomimus was an omnivore: it ate animals and plants. Its long claws could hook leaves and fruit from low trees. It also fed on insects and lizards.

MAKE A MEAT-EATER'S TOOTH

Model a big ball of self-hardening clay into the shape of a meat-eating dinosaur's tooth. Texture the surface and mark it so that it looks ancient and fossilized. It may take up to two days for the tooth to harden. When it is hard, paint your ferocious tooth.

Baryonyx claw

Tyrannosaurus tooth

△ **Baryonyx** had long, curved thumb-claws. Tyrannosaurus had enormous teeth. They were up to 18 cm long, with sharp edges like steak knives. Tooth finds have helped to tell us what different dinosaurs fed on.

The Age of the Dinosaurs is divided into three periods: the Triassic (240-205 million years ago), the Jurassic (205-138 million years ago) and the Cretaceous period (138-65 million years ago).

▷ **Tyrannosaurus** was about 12 m long and weighed over 6 tonnes. Its forward-facing eyes helped it to judge distance well as it moved in to attack smaller dinosaurs. Its tiny arms look feeble but held sharp claws.

Plant-eating Dinosaurs

Which had the longest neck?
Mamenchisaurus, a huge plant-eater found in China, had the longest neck of any animal ever known. Its neck was 15 m long - longer than eight tall men lying head to toe!

The dinosaur herbivores, or plant-eaters, fed on the vegetation they could reach. Small herbivores ate roots and plants on the ground, and others may have reared up on their back legs to reach higher leaves.

The long-necked sauropods, such as Diplodocus, were tall enough to reach the treetops. These huge animals must have spent nearly all their time eating.

NEW WORDS

herbivore A vegetarian animal that eats only plants.

rear up To raise itself on its back legs.

stud A curved lump or knob.

vegetation Living plants, including twigs and the leaves of trees.

Scutellosaurus was a tiny plant-eater, about the size of a modern cat. It had rows of bony studs along its back and tail, to protect it from attack by any larger meat-eaters. It could walk or run on its back legs, as well as on all fours.

IGUANODON

This large, heavy dinosaur was a peaceful plant-eater that could stand and walk either on its back legs or on all fours. It had spiked thumbs, which it may have used to defend itself if it was attacked by a hungry meat-eater.

◁ **Long-necked plant-eaters** may also have reared up to reach even higher treetops. Diplodocus picked leaves off with its front teeth, but had no back teeth for chewing.

The huge shoulder bones of Ultrasaurus were 2.7 m long, much longer than the tallest human. Its hip bones were also bigger than a man. Ultrasaurus was about 30 m long.

DIG UP A DIPLODOCUS

Cut up straws for bones and make them into a complete skeleton on a cardboard base. Brush each straw with PVA glue and fix them firmly into position. Leave the straws to dry, and then brush more glue between the bones and around the whole skeleton. Sprinkle all over with sand. After a few minutes, tip the surplus sand onto newspaper. Then you'll have your very own fossilized Diplodocus!

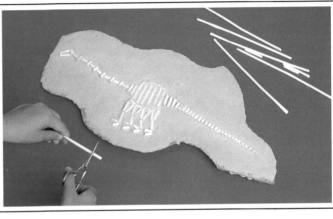

▽ **Diplodocus** was about 27 m long and weighed 12 tonnes. Its bones have been found in the western USA, and the first skeleton was discovered in Wyoming in 1899. Its whiplash tail was even longer than its neck and was made up of over 80 bones.

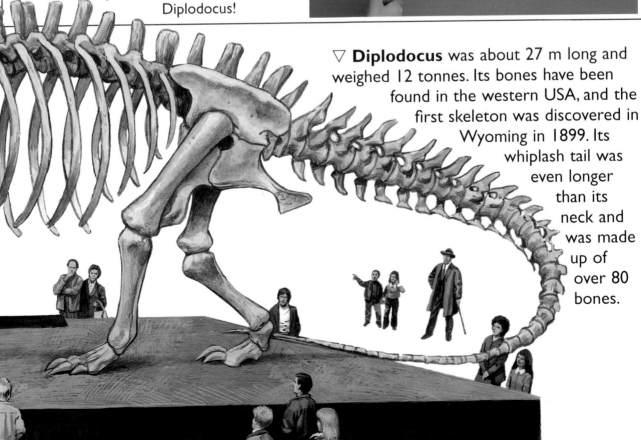

Warm- or Cold-Blooded Creatures?

Today's reptiles are cold-blooded. This means their body warmth changes with the temperature of their surroundings. Scientists used to think dinosaurs were cold-blooded. But were they?

In recent years it has been suggested that many or even all dinosaurs were warm-blooded. If they were, it meant that their bodies stayed constantly warm because they got heat and energy from the food they ate. It certainly seems that dinosaurs did not cool down and become slower like a modern-day reptile.

▽ **The cold-blooded Komodo dragon** is the biggest lizard alive today. It grows up to 3 m long.

△ **If plant-eaters,** like this Lufengosaurus, were warm-blooded, they must have eaten vast amounts of food. Or perhaps they were cold-blooded?

Cold-blooded reptiles have to wait for the sun to warm them up each morning before they can move about. This puts them in danger.

A cold-blooded Komodo dragon needs its own weight in food every two months. A warm-blooded lion needs its own weight in food every week. Warm-blooded animals need to eat more food so that they can keep warm.

NEW WORDS
cold-blooded With a blood temperature that varies with the temperature outside.
plated Covered with bony plates.
warm-blooded With a body temperature that always stays the same.

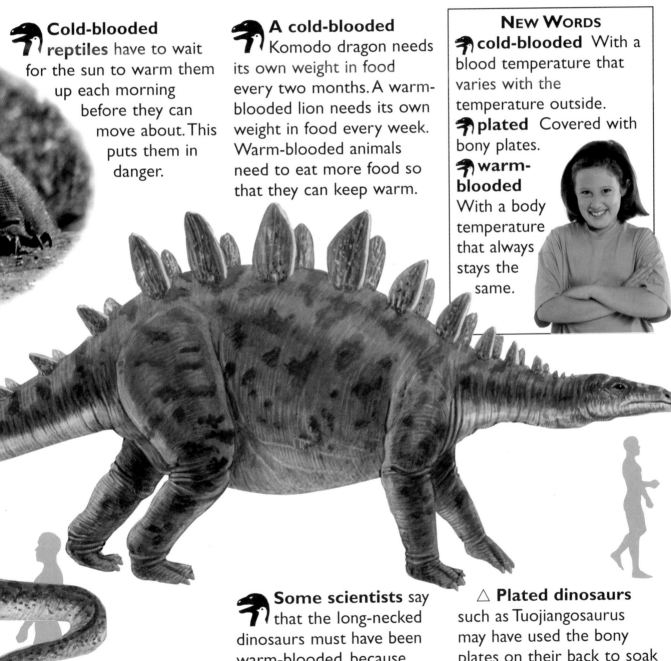

Some scientists say that the long-necked dinosaurs must have been warm-blooded, because they would need such high blood pressure to get the blood up to their brain.

△ **Plated dinosaurs** such as Tuojiangosaurus may have used the bony plates on their back to soak up the sun's heat and warm themselves up. So they may have been cold-blooded.

23

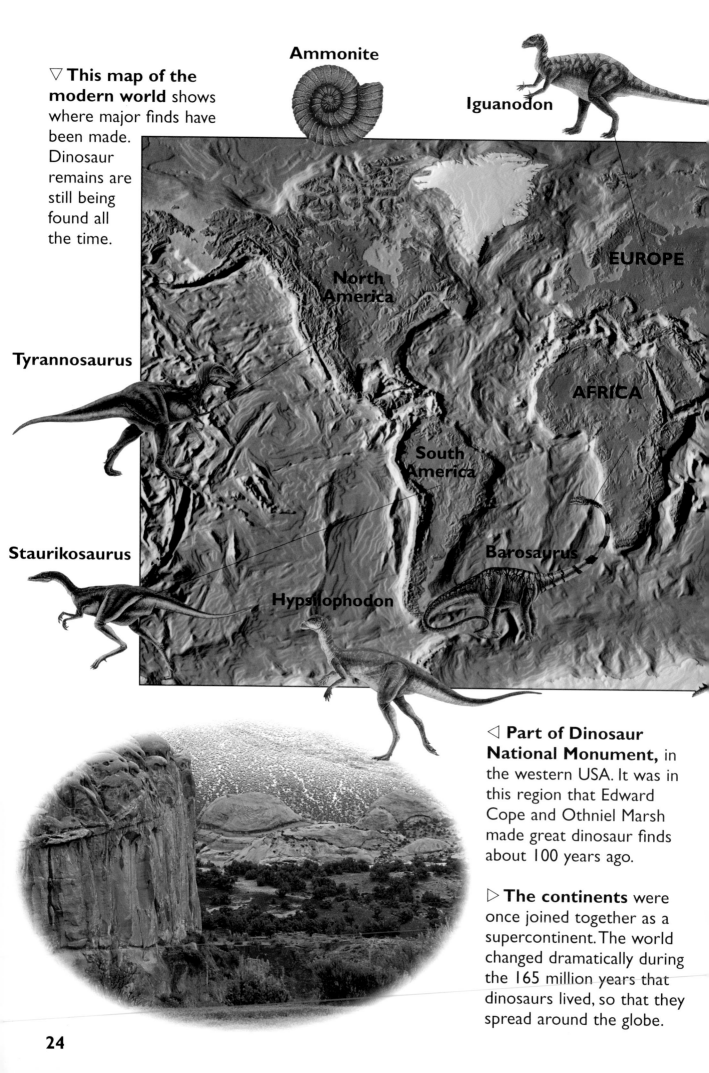

Ammonite

Iguanodon

▽ **This map of the modern world** shows where major finds have been made. Dinosaur remains are still being found all the time.

North America

EUROPE

AFRICA

South America

Tyrannosaurus

Staurikosaurus

Barosaurus

Hypsilophodon

◁ **Part of Dinosaur National Monument,** in the western USA. It was in this region that Edward Cope and Othniel Marsh made great dinosaur finds about 100 years ago.

▷ **The continents** were once joined together as a supercontinent. The world changed dramatically during the 165 million years that dinosaurs lived, so that they spread around the globe.

Where Dinosaurs Lived

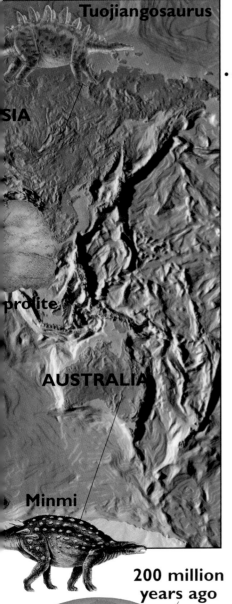

Tuojiangosaurus

SIA

prolite

AUSTRALIA

Minmi

Dinosaur remains have been found all over the world. In fact, similar dinosaurs have been found on different continents, yet we know that they were land animals and could not have swum across vast oceans.

During the Age of Dinosaurs the continents were slowly drifting apart from the original supercontinent. So the dinosaurs could have crossed from one continent to another by land early on.

NEW WORDS
🌀 **Coprolites** Fossilized animal droppings.
🌀 **supercontinent** The huge mass of land that once existed. The individual continents split off from this mass.

200 million years ago

100 million years ago

Today

▽ **Famous dinosaur collectors:** 1 Dr Robert Plot; 2 Mary Mantell; 3 Dr Gideon Mantell; 4 Sir Richard Owen; 5 Edward Cope; 6 Othniel Marsh.

Moving Herds

We have learned a lot about how dinosaurs lived from the discovery of fossil footprints. These show how dinosaurs moved, and whether they travelled alone, in small groups or in larger herds.

Apatosaurus was one of the large plant-eaters. From footprints found in Texas, USA, we know that these dinosaurs roamed across the North American plains in herds. The footprints were all made at the same time, 150 million years ago.

Herds of up to 100 plant-eaters may have travelled long distances in search of food. Some tracks have shown that smaller and younger dinosaurs walked in the middle of the herd, so that they were safe from any attack.

MAKING FOOTPRINTS
Pour paint into a baking tin or something similar. Put this at one end of some spread-out newspapers, and put a bucket of water and a towel at the other end. Then step into the paint, walk across the paper, and wash your feet in the water. Ask a friend to do the same, so that you can compare prints.

△ **These dinosaur tracks** were found in Queensland, Australia. At the time of the dinosaurs, the continent of Australia was moving away from Antarctica.

▽ **Dinosaurs** such as Parasaurolophus and Saurolophus had head balloons and crests. They may have used these to increase the noises they made to warn other herd members.

▽ **A herd of Apatosaurus** on the move. For many years, most scientists thought that these dinosaurs lived in water, using their long neck like a snorkel. The footprint finds proved this to be quite wrong.

Scientists think that Apatosaurus may have been able to travel at a similar speed to modern elephants. But a huge Brachiosaurus probably only moved at a slow walk of about 5 kph or so.

▽ **Hypsilophodon** were small, fast plant-eaters. Remains of herds have been found. The first known Hypsilophodon was found in 1849, but at that time it was wrongly thought to be a common Iguanodon.

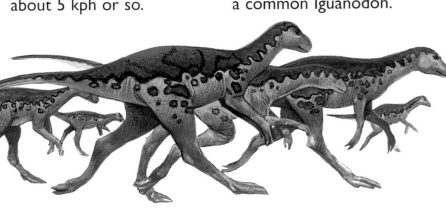

NEW WORDS

crest A bony bump on top of a dinosaur's head; some crests were big and might have been used in signalling.

head balloon A flap of skin on top of a dinosaur's head, that blew up just like a balloon.

MOVING AROUND

The Tarbosaurus found in China is so similar to the Tyrannosaurus found in North America that they must be very close relatives. Perhaps they simply travelled in different directions.

Tarbosaurus

Tyrannosaurus

Eggs and Nests

Female dinosaurs laid eggs, just like modern reptiles. The eggs were leathery and hard-shelled, which gave them protection. They were often laid in mud nests or hollows. Then the mothers covered them with plants or sand. We know all this from the fossilized eggs that have been found. The first of these was discovered in the Gobi Desert in Mongolia in 1923. We also know that some groups of dinosaurs built their nests close together, in colonies. Scientists think that some dinosaurs returned to the same nesting place year after year. Some dinosaur mothers stayed by their nests to look after the eggs and the new baby dinosaurs.

△ **These tiny Protoceratops** are hatching from their eggs. Their mother is close by, and she may have stayed to help feed and protect her young until they were able to fend for themselves - about 80 million years ago.

Male and female dinosaurs may have looked different, especially in their colouring. Two slightly different kinds of the same dinosaur have been found. These might have been male and female.

MAKE A NEST OF EGGS

First roll self-hardening clay into oval egg shapes, and then let them dry. If you want to make a really big dinosaur egg, screw old newspaper into a ball before covering it with clay and smearing any joins together with water. Mould the clay into an egg shape and let it dry. Then you could paint the eggs whatever colour you think they might have been. Finally, when the paint is dry, put your dinosaur eggs together in a nest made of sand.

◁ **Today's crocodiles** behave in a way which is probably very similar to dinosaurs. They make nests and cover them over with plants and mud, which help keep the eggs warm. When the babies hatch, mother carries them gently in her jaws to a nearby pool.

How big?
The biggest dinosaur eggs found so far were 30 cm long - only about six times bigger than a chicken's egg. The rapid growth of hatched babies is one reason for thinking that dinosaurs were warm-blooded.

NEW WORDS
🖘 **hatch** To break out of an egg.
🖘 **colony** A group of animals who live together.
🖘 **leathery** Tough and flexible, like animal skin.

▽ **Maiasaura,** which means "good mother lizard", was so named when a group of its nests were found with fossilized eggs, and some babies, still inside them. The mothers would have scooped out mud nests about 2 m across and laid up to 20 eggs inside, each about 20 cm long. They then covered the eggs up.

Helmets, Spines and Armour

Big, slow-moving animals need to protect themselves against fast, fierce meat-eaters. Many plant-eating dinosaurs had some form of armour-plating to offer this protection.

Some dinosaurs had plates and spines running down their back and tail. Others had spikes that grew in their skin. They even had a bony club at the end of their tail, which was a powerful weapon against attackers. One group of dinosaurs had thick, bony skulls, which they used to head-butt each other during fights.

△ **The largest** bone-headed dinosaur, Pachycephalosaurus, had a thick, dome-shaped skull. This head-butting creature was 4.6 m long.

Styracosaurus lived on Earth about 75 million years ago, and fossils have been found in the USA and Canada.

Triceratops' teeth were hard on one side. The other, softer side wore down faster, leaving a sharp cutting edge.

Stegosaurus was about 9 m long, but it had a small head and its brain was little bigger than a walnut. Dinosaurs' skulls were filled mainly with muscle and bone.

△ **Styracosaurus** had long spikes sticking out of a bony frill. It also had a large nose horn, like a modern rhinoceros.

CARD STEGOSAURUS

Cut the sides off some large cardboard boxes and tape them together. Draw the long dinosaur body shape of a Stegosaurus (see the photograph, right) and cut it out. Make plates and tail spikes from card, and use eggcups for scales. Paint the eggcups green and stick them on the body. Fasten the plates with tape. Screw up lots of pieces of tissue paper and glue them all over your dinosaur's body. You could use a bottle top for a beady, prehistoric eye!

◁ **Triceratops** means "three-horned face". Although the horns were for self-defence, scientists think that these dinosaurs may also have fought one another.

△ **Euoplocephalus** had slabs of bony armour, spikes on its back and a clubbed tail. It used its powerful muscles to swing its tail at any enemies.

NEW WORDS

armour A protective covering for the body.

club Something heavy, like a tail, that can be used as a weapon.

frill A fold of skin and bone for protection around the neck.

head-butt To use its head to hit another dinosaur on the head.

Other Giant Reptiles

During the long Age of Dinosaurs, other giant reptiles lived in the world's oceans.

Like their dinosaur cousins, sea reptiles breathed air. This meant that they had to come to the surface regularly to fill their lungs. Sea reptiles such as the plesiosaurs and pliosaurs might have laid their eggs in sandy nests on the shore. Although they, too, were reptiles, ichthyosaurs gave birth to live young at sea.

All these giant reptiles died out, but smaller crocodiles and turtles still exist today.

▽ **Tanystrophaeus** was a land animal, but it used its long, thin neck to catch fish underwater. Shonisaurus was the largest ichthyosaur, growing up to 15 m long.

Tanystrophaeus

Shonisaurus

32

Nessie the plesiosaur?
People who claim to have seen the Loch Ness monster describe it very much like a long-necked plesiosaur such as Elasmosaurus. But all efforts to track down the "monster" have so far failed.

▽ **Elasmosaurus** was about 13 m in length, making it the longest of the long-necked plesiosaurs. Kronosaurus was a huge pliosaur with massive, sharp teeth. And Archelon was a giant turtle, almost 4 m long. All three sea reptiles lived towards the end of the Age of Dinosaurs.

Their air-filled lungs made it very difficult for plesiosaurs to dive deep under water to catch their prey. To weigh themselves down and make things easier, they seem to have swallowed stones. Crocodiles do exactly the same today.

△ **Deinosuchus** was the largest crocodile that ever lived. It was up to 12 m long and had massive jaws. It swam in rivers and swamps, and might have fed on land animals coming there to drink.

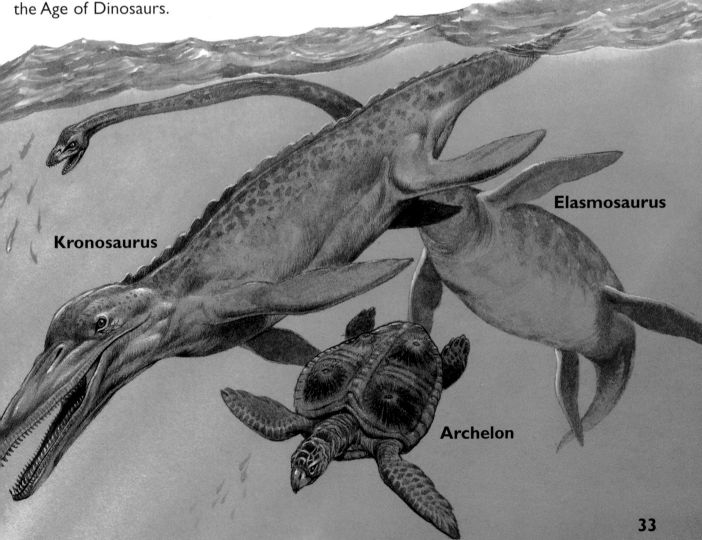

Kronosaurus

Elasmosaurus

Archelon

Into the Air

Reptiles took to the air over 200 million years ago. While dinosaurs ruled the land, pterosaurs controlled the skies long before the first birds took off.

Pterosaurs flew on wings of skin, which stretched out from their bodies, along their arms to their long fingers. They launched themselves from high cliffs and flapped their wings as they rode the air currents. They had light, delicate bones, which made it easier for them to stay in the air.

▽ **Pteranodons** flew over the seas and used their long, toothless beaks to catch fish. They had a wing span of more than 5 m. The long bony crest at the back of it's head may have been used as a rudder, to guide and balance the pteranodon as it flew.

Fossils of Pteranodon have been dated at about 80 million years old.

EARLY GLIDERS

Icarosaurus and Coelurosauravus were early lizard-like animals with wings. Icarosaurus lived over 200 million years ago. It climbed trees, with its wings folded against its body. Then it launched itself off, and its thin wings helped it glide through the air

Icarosaurus

Coelurosauravus

NEW WORDS

glide To travel through the air using natural air currents instead of wing-power.

pterosaur A flying reptile that existed at the same time as the dinosaurs.

rudder Something that helps in steering.

34

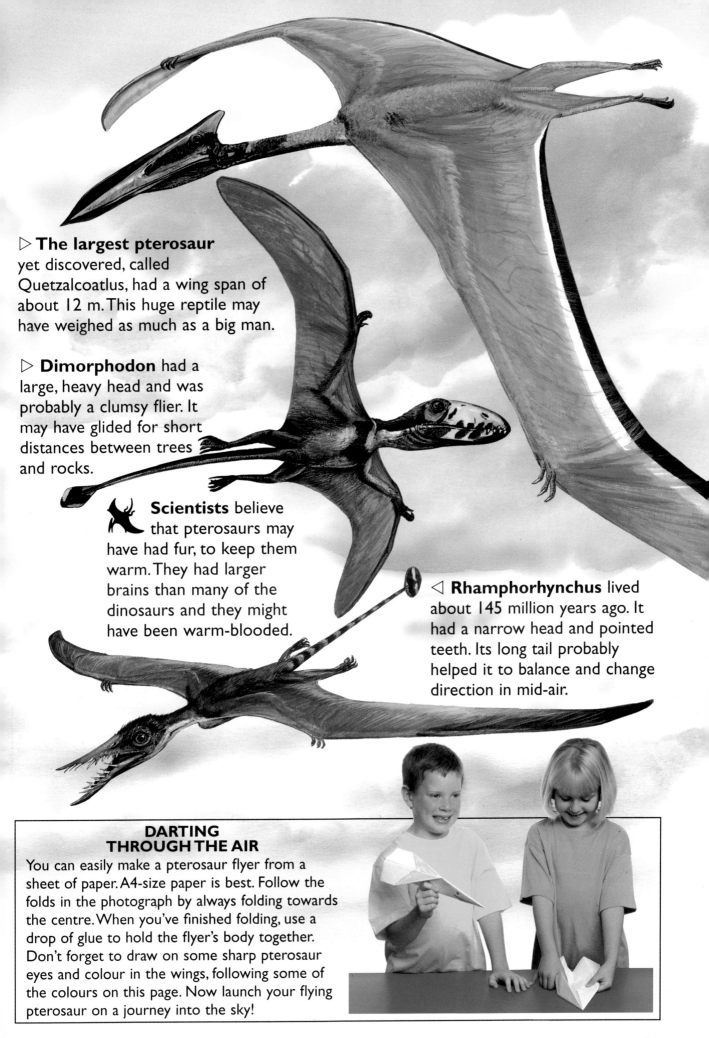

▷ **The largest pterosaur** yet discovered, called Quetzalcoatlus, had a wing span of about 12 m. This huge reptile may have weighed as much as a big man.

▷ **Dimorphodon** had a large, heavy head and was probably a clumsy flier. It may have glided for short distances between trees and rocks.

Scientists believe that pterosaurs may have had fur, to keep them warm. They had larger brains than many of the dinosaurs and they might have been warm-blooded.

◁ **Rhamphorhynchus** lived about 145 million years ago. It had a narrow head and pointed teeth. Its long tail probably helped it to balance and change direction in mid-air.

DARTING THROUGH THE AIR

You can easily make a pterosaur flyer from a sheet of paper. A4-size paper is best. Follow the folds in the photograph by always folding towards the centre. When you've finished folding, use a drop of glue to hold the flyer's body together. Don't forget to draw on some sharp pterosaur eyes and colour in the wings, following some of the colours on this page. Now launch your flying pterosaur on a journey into the sky!

The First Birds

The first known bird lived about 150 million years ago. Scientists think that it was closely related to the dinosaurs, and in many ways it was very much like a reptile.

We call this first bird Archaeopteryx, which means "ancient wing". Unlike the pterosaurs, Archaeopteryx's body was covered with feathers. But scientists think it might not have been able to fly very well.

Around 90 million years ago, while dinosaurs still roamed the land, water birds were starting to catch fish in the sea. Some of these flying creatures may still have been more at home in the water than they were on land or in the air.

What colour?
We don't know what colour the first birds were. Fossil feathers show us shape and size, but not colour. Males and females may have had different colours.

△ **Diatryma** was a fast-running flightless bird with a large, parrot-like beak and big claws. It was as big as a tall human and lived about 50 million years ago. Diatryma might have chased the first small horses.

▽ **Hesperornis** was a good underwater swimmer, but probably couldn't fly. Ichthyornis was like a modern gull and could fly to catch fish.

Hesperornis

Ichthyornis

▷ **These bones of a Hypacrosaurus,** plant-eating dinosaur, show the shape of the animal very clearly. The bones are usually found near each other, but often have to be put together like a jigsaw.

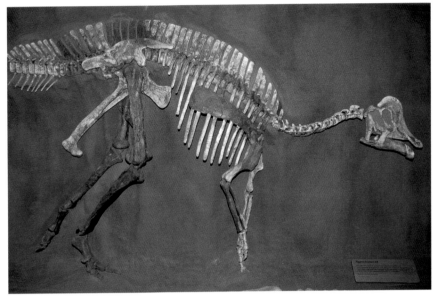

▽ **First dirt has to be brushed** from bones. Then each bone is labelled and given a number. This helps when putting the pieces together later.

▽ **Palaeontologists** keep detailed notes on where bones were found. They take photographs and make drawings and diagrams before the bones are taken away from the original site. Other scientists can learn a lot from these original notes.

▽ **Bones are carefully wrapped** in wet plaster before they are moved from the original site. When the plaster has hardened, the bones can safely be taken to a laboratory. The plaster jacket that protected them can then be taken off, so that scientists can test and study the bones.

NEW WORDS

🦴 **laboratory** The place where a scientist works and does experiments.

🦴 **palaeontologist** A scientist who studies fossils.

🦴 **plaster** A soft paste that hardens when it is left to dry.

Quiz

1. **What shape** is a starfish? *(page 8)*

2. **How many different kinds** of seaweed are there? *(page 9)*

3. **Which famous scientist** travelled to South America in 1832? *(page 10)*

4. **What was the name** of Charles Darwin's ship? *(page 11)*

5. **Where do amphibians** lay their eggs? *(page 12)*

6. **Which is the largest amphibian** alive today? *(page 13)*

7. **What does the name reptile** come from? *(page 14)*

8. **What did sail-backed reptiles** use their sail for? *(page 15)*

9. **Which animals** are the two types of dinosaur hips named after? *(page 16)*

10. **When did the first dinosaurs** appear on Earth? *(page 17)*

11. **What was the name** of an egg-snatching dinosaur? *(page 18)*

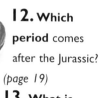

12. **Which period** comes after the Jurassic? *(page 19)*

13. **What is** a herbivore? *(page 20)*

14. **How long** was Diplodocus? *(page 21)*

15. **Which is the biggest** lizard alive today? *(page 22)*

16. **What warms reptiles** up each morning? *(page 23)*

17. **Where did the famous dinosaur** collectors Cope and Marsh make great finds? *(page 24)*

18. **What do we call the huge mass** of land that the continents split from? *(page 25)*

19. **Why did young dinosaurs** walk in the middle of the herd? *(page 26)*

20. **What did footprints** tell us about Apatosaurus? *(page 27)*

21. **Where were the first dinosaur** eggs found? *(page 28)*

22. **What does the name** "Maiasaura" mean? *(page 29)*

23. **What was special** about Pachycephalosaurus' head? *(page 30)*

24. **Which dinosaur** had a "three-horned face"? *(page 31)*

25. **Which had a longer neck,** a plesiosaur or a pliosaur? *(page 32)*

26. **What did plesiosaurs swallow** to weigh them down? *(page 33)*

27. **Did pterosaurs have** feathers? *(page 34)*

28. **How big was the wing** span of the largest pterosaur? *(page 35)*

29. **When did** the first bird live? *(page 36)*

30. **What did Archaeopteryx** use its claws for? *(page 37)*

31. **Where is** Meteor Crater? *(page 38)*

32. **When did** dinosaurs die out? *(page 39)*

33. **Which modern animal** is similar to the very early mammals? *(page 40)*

34. **What did Uintatherium** have on its head? *(page 41)*

35. **Who do we think** was first to use fire? *(page 42)*

36. **Which came first,** "upright man" or "handy man"? *(page 43)*

37. **Were there humans alive** at the same time as dinosaurs? *(page 44)*

38. **What do scientists wrap** dinosaur bones in? *(page 45)*

Index

ACKNOWLEDGEMENTS

The publishers wish to thank the following artists who have contributed
to this book:

Mike Foster (The Maltings Partnership) 9 (CL), 14 (BL), 17 (CB, BL),
18 (CR), 20 (TL), 23 (BL, BR), 29 (CL), 33 (TL), 36 (CL),
38 (CL), caption icons thoughout;
Steve Kirk 9 (TL), 15 (B), 19 (BR), 34 (TR, C), 35 (T, C, B), 38-39 (B);
Mel Pickering (Contour Publishing) 16 (TL), 19 (CT), 24 (T), 25(C), 44 (B);
Terry Riley Page 8 (BL), 10-11 (B), 12-13 (B), 17 (CB, BL), 18 (BL), 20 (TR),
27 (T), 32-33 (B), 36 (B), 41 (T, CT, TR);
Michael White (Temple Rogers) 10 (CR), 11 (T), 15 (CR), 20-21 (CB),
23 (CL, CR), 25 (BR), 26 (BR), 29 (B), 33 (TR), 34 (B), 40-41 (B).

The publishers wish to thank the following for supplying photographs
for this book:

Corbis 9 (B), 37 (B), 38 (TR), 44 (TR), 45 (TR);
Miles Kelly Archives 8 (TL), 9 (TR), 11 (CL, CR), 13 (TR), 16-17 (CB), 18 (CT),
21 (T), 22 (CR, B), 23 (CB), 24 (TR, C, CL, CB, CR), 25 (TL, CL), 27 (BL, BR),
30 (TL, BL), 30-31 (B), 31 (C), 37 (T), 39 (CR), 40 (TR), 42 (BR);
Natural Science Photos 16 (BL), 17 (TR), 24 (BL), 26 (TR), 29 (T), 39 (CL),
45 (CL, CR, BL).
All model photography by **Mike Perry at David Lipson Photography Ltd.**

Models in this series:
Lisa Anness, Sophie Clark, Alison Cobb, Edward Delaney, Elizabeth Fallas,
Ryan French, Luke Gilder, Lauren May Headley, Christie Hooper, Caroline Kelly,
Alice McGhee, Daniel Melling, Ryan Oyeyemi, Aaron Phipps,
Eriko Sato, Jack Wallace.

Clothes for model photography supplied by:
Adams Children's Wear